Yours And Mine

A love story in verse

Prerna Kashyap

BookLeaf Publishing

India | USA | UK

Made with ❤ on the BookLeaf Publishing Platform
www.bookleafpub.in
www.bookleafpub.com

Dedication

For Animesh
This is as much yours as it is mine

Preface

How do thoughts convey,
In an unassuming way?

Sometimes when nothing is said,
Or when the written word is read.

A few words hold multitudes,
A concoction of ideas brewed,

For the reader to partake,
A reward for the poet's aches...

Acknowledgements

Thank you to my mother for a lifetime of belief and strength. To my father and sisters for support. To my daughter Ananya, for helping me keep it real. To my son Bhuvan, for his loving hugs. To my husband Animesh, for picking up the slack, for giving me time and always believing in me.

And to you, dear Reader, for being a part of this journey.

1. The Windowpane

(He)

How long have I travelled?
How far have I come?
The reward for my struggles
Is a steady income.

It's almost been a year
Since I came from the plains
To this land of drear
Cold, and heavy rains.

Today when it rained
It snowed a bit too.
Across a windowpane
Was where I saw you.

How alluring was
Your innocent face!
The frost on the glass
Like an intricate lace.

The window's iron frame
Completed the picture.

It's etched on my brain
For now and for ever.

May be 'twas the cold,
Maybe 'twas the snow,
I heard something untold
Like I'd never heard before.

'Take another peek,
Steal another glance,
Here's what you seek,
And this is your chance!'

I stepped across the street
Into the quaint shop,
Where they served tea
In tiny earthen pots.

Were they mere seconds
Or was it a lifetime?
As my heart beckoned
To claim what was mine.

2. Tea

(She)

The skies changed hue
And temperature dipped,
A chilling wind blew
Freezing my fingertips.

The willows outside whistled
In the cold dark night,
Shopkeepers gained a little
By the customers' plight.

And then when you came
In our shop and sneezed,
All drenched from the rain
And trembling like a leaf.

I couldn't help but meet
Your intense gaze.
I felt weak in the knees
Your eyes were ablaze.

You weren't from here
I could tell at a glance.

You were dark and appeared
Like a mystery man.

You sat yourself down
And suffered quietly.
Then slightly frowned
As I brought you tea.

'Warm yourself up,' I said,
'Or you're going to be sick.'
You complained instead,
'I never ordered this.'

I was visibly flustered
And a little bit miffed
You were stingy and absurd,
So I couldn't resist.

'Why else come,' I snapped
'If not for the tea?'
'Why else?' you asked,
'Why else, indeed.'

3. Cigarettes

(He)

It's been a week
Of heavy snowfall,
The nights are bleak
With sudden rain squalls.

The pipes have frozen
And the power is out.
There's frankly no reason
To be up and about,

Except at the office I'm
Swamped with work.
Reports and flim-flam
On taxes and perks.

I can't wrap my head
Around an audit sheet;
I'd rather walk instead
On the desolate streets.

Heaters and briquettes
Give a moment's warmth,

I buy a pack of cigarettes
To feel less forlorn.

Dismally, I light one
And take a long drag.
It fires me from within
Like nothing else can.

But then I see you
Near the mini bus stop,
With your cap askew
Munching a corn cob.

You wear a red shawl
And look like a peach;
I am so enthralled
As though high on hashish.

You walk towards me
With a friend in tow.
I puff deliberately
Taking nice and slow.

I wait for your smile,
I wait for your frown,
The way you beguile
Even when you scowl.

Your eyes shoot daggers
At me and you grimace,
While I soon thereafter
 Stub out the cigarette.

Then you relax and
Casually move on.
Nothing really said
But the heart goes on.

4. Corn on the Cob

(She)

The college reopened
After the winter break,
My heavy boots thunk
On the frozen lake.

The snow drapes trees
Like a white fur cloak,
Boughs bend at the knees
Wanting in on the joke.

'You've put on weight,'
The winter wind says
'You shouldn't stand straight
But move and sway.'

'Every now and then
When the sun shines,
I shed some of it
So don't you whine,'

So reply the trees
Standing tall with grace,

Making symphonies
And singing its praise.

How lovely is winter!
How serene the scene!
But I feel tethered
As if caught between

Days spent in college
And evenings at the shop.
These are places in which
I see new faces a lot.

Every now and then
I meet people I know,
But I didn't see you again
After the first snow.

Were you just a tourist
Or here for some work?
With a fleeting interest
To buy some merch.

An old woman sits
By a lighted coal fire,
I get cozy by bits,
Standing next to a briar.

As the heat ascends
From coal to the corns,
A waft of grassy scent
Is suddenly airborne.

Why, roasted corn cob
With a smearing of salt,
'n lemon brushed on top
Is perfect to a fault!

I wrap my shawl tight
Around my freezing arms,
And take a big bite
Of the bright yellow corns.

And there at a distance
Is that you I see?
Is it happenstance
That yet again we meet?

Leaning against a wall
Making rings from smoke.
What a Neanderthal
I think, and then choke.

But you look at me

With such a lazy smile,
I'm flummoxed, really
And it takes me a while

To realize I'm blushing.
So I frown and glare
Then you stop smoking
As if I care.

5. The Bench

(He)

The town's holding a fair
For a local deity,
The paved central square
Bustles with activity.

The place has witnessed
Many historical events,
The customs here must
Be its cultural strength.

The large open space
Is lined with small shops -
From trendy cafes
To selling wooden pots.

There's a huge crowd
Around a tableau,
I push and plough
My way through.

The ridge has been lined
With a wrought iron fence,

Under a pine tree I find
An ornate iron bench.

The bench is a remnant
Of the eighteenth century,
But due to inclement
Weather is a bit rusty.

You sit on this bench
That was made for two,
I take a step herehence
And sit down next to you.

6. Your Name

(She)

For years I've been
Coming to the local fair,
The town and its kin
Are all present here.

My family, my friends
And distant relatives,
Pray and burn incense
For making merits.

I am in awe of our
Myths and legends,
How kingdoms waver
When Gods upend.

I bow and pray
Before our deity,
And then slip away
To enjoy the festivity.

I look at knickknacks
Displayed in the stalls,

But the prices with tax
Have me appalled.

So I buy nothing
And tiredly walk away,
As I bruised my shin
Earlier in the day.

I see an old pine
Shadowing a bench,
And proceed to recline,
Devoid of any strength.

Then out of nowhere,
You're sitting beside me.
How? When? Why here?
Why must you baffle me?

You give me your name,
And then ask me mine.
At first, it was strange,
But we talked for sometime.

I am not really aware
Of all that was said,
But hours later ,
When I lay in my bed,

I call out your name
In a slight whisper.
Then with a claim,
Aloud and clear.

I try writing it down
On a paper,
Then add my own
A while later.

7. Bus Ride

(He)

I really can't get
Used to the snow,
Everything is wet
From floor to door.

My fingers are swollen
Because of the cold,
I nick my face often;
Shaving's such a chore!

My washing hasn't dried
And my clothes smell bad,
There's shortage of supplies
But I make do with that.

If it were up to me,
I would surely hibernate.
However, lately
I've let, my heart dictate.

I weather the wretched
Cold, to be with you.

So I'm blindly headed
To terminal number two.

You take a bus home
From this stop each day.
I dash and I bolt
To board it right away.

I have half a mind
To act chivalrously,
You smile like sunshine
When you see me.

So I sit myself down
In the seat next to you.
'The cut is purple-brown,'
You say, 'And I'm all blue.'

You point at my face
And then I understand.
'Your concern is misplaced,'
I say, and take your hand.

Holding hands amounts
To being fixed like a rivet,
The warmth is tantamount
To smoking a cigarette.

Within bits of dialogue
A longing has begun.
That's what comes of
Loving someone.

8. A Day's Growth of Beard

(She)

I rather treasure
Our daily bus rides;
There's nothing better
Than sitting by your side.

To tell you the truth
I'm not myself now.
Is it a folly of youth
That makes me doubt?

I can't seem to move
When you're not around.
My family would disapprove
If ever they found.

I've become such a sop
The kind I deplore,
So I mentally vow not
To love you anymore.

Today you wear a jacket
And a day's growth of beard.

You've become a habit;
It's even worse than I feared.

I try to act aloof
Because this isn't right!
I'll get over you,
I try with all my might.

The more I restrain,
The more I reveal,
My efforts are in vain,
For I can't conceal.

That all I want to do,
Is to touch your face,
And then snugly hold you,
In a warm embrace.

Your soft stubble
Is just within my reach...
You save me the trouble,
And give a peck on my cheek.

9. The Wait

(He)

I wanted to be there
For your special day,
But work interfered
And I had to go away

To a branch office.
There's been a fire
On the premises
It's a legal quagmire,

A financial setback
For the company.
We're holding back
For the insurers' scrutiny.

After five days
Of crisis management,
Assessing the stakes,
Making up for damage done,

My work here is over;
Now I'm heading back.

I've pain in my shoulder
'n drive into a cul-de-sac

It's a three hour drive
By the company car,
But it takes me five
As I often miss the mark.

I silently curse myself
For making you wait,
Due to the cold spell
It's hard to concentrate.

It's already past midnight
When I reach home.
It's late so I leave a
Message on your phone.

The ache in my shoulder
Is much worse now.
My room seems colder
As I make do without

Hearing your voice,
Or a word from you.
But I hardly have a choice
And the wait continues...

10. My Special Day

(She)

Grandma taught me weaving,
When I was but a child.
Despite rural upbringing,
I was gleefully styled

My feet pedal to warp,
My hands move the weft,
The yarn moves forth,
Then to the right and left.

Until I find the rhythm,
To compose the weave,
Include geometric pattern,
Or flowers and leaves.

It's either in my head,
Or in handwritten scrawl.
Lately I'm being fetched
For my colorful shawls.

They say that I'm part
Of a documentary

On 'Youth and Craft:
An artistic legacy'

To say that I'm thrilled,
Is an understatement
Why, this could just be
My rise to eminence!

I'm the chosen one
Being noted for her skill!
You're the first person
I share my news with.

I ask you to be with me
On the day of shoot.
Not to friends or family,
Do I vaguely allude

I wait the entire day,
And you never show.
May be you're waylaid,
But it's hard to let go.

The filming went well,
I'm sure I made the grade,
But it does nothing to dispel,
That you rained on my parade.

11. My Room

(He)

I lay awake in bed
For a long time,
Waiting for your text –
Disgruntled or benign

I'm overcome with fatigue,
My text is still unread,
May be you're asleep
Or just really upset.

I know I let you down,
And that I hurt you.
Can't we talk about it now?
Isn't it long overdue?

I'm gleaming with sweat
When I wake up at noon,
Then right out of a dream
You walk into my room.

'How did you,' I ask
'Manage to come here?'

'Don't look so shocked,
Silly, we talked earlier,'

You say with concern,
'You've fallen ill
After your sojourn,
You better rest until

The fever comes down.'
You cook me hot soup
And order me around,
All earnest and resolute.

My cramped cold room
Is filled with your warmth,
You're my bloom,
I pull you in my arms.

'You're innately woven
In the fabric of my life,
For all I've done and haven't
I truly apologize,'

I say and gently plant
A kiss on your lips,
Then curiously I want
A lot more than this.

You strike my shoulder
With a knockout punch,
'You rascal! Smoker! Poser!
All wrapped-in-one!'

I grimace with pain
And falter back a step,
You get that it's unfeigned
And again start to fret.

I rejoice in your worry
In spite of the ache,
Just to have you near me
I'll give it all it takes.

12. The Kiss

(She)

Your voice was groggy
On the phone earlier,
You've probably
Come down with fever.

Although I'm aggrieved,
And have a bone to pick
With you, I'll not proceed,
Not while you're sick.

You're the reason,
I ought to be admonished.
I lied to everyone,
Sneaked away from college.

I trudge uphill,
Wandering through alleys,
Because you live
Far above the valley.

Am I am wrong perhaps?
Is my visit opportune?

A narrow paved path
Leads me to your room.

There's an air of gloom
With signs of neglect,
Your clothes are strewn
Where books are kept.

Placed against a wall,
Is a narrow bed,
You're lying in a sprawl,
Like a train-wreck,

I forget my ill-will,
And rush to your side.
You're green around the gills,
And give me a fright.

I chop, sauté, boil
Vegetables in a pot,
The fruit of my toil
Is a soup piping hot.

You feel much better
After eating the soup,
I pick up the litter
And tidy up your room.

Suddenly I'm aware
I'm alone with you,
I fidget with my hair,
Don't know what to do.

You whisper sweet nothings
And even apologize,
You have me blushing
With your lingering eyes,

Then you press your lips,
Firmly against mine.
How reality slips
Is hard to divine.

13. Disgruntled

(He)

Ever since you walked in
On my solitude,
I've just been waiting,
Waiting for you.

Now that I've held you
Close, in my arms,
My heart keeps looking
For your warmth.

You've turned my life
Upside down,
Everything that's mine,
Everything I own.

The other day you visited
My place on a whim,
Wasn't it an invisible
Line you crossed then?

Since you have caused
Such a tumult,

Shouldn't you have paused
To be responsible?

But you go on as is
With your life,
With no other meetings,
Save the public bus rides.

What am I to do
But lie in wait?
For a brief tryst or,
A moment intimate.

14. Confused

(She)

Lately you've been
A bit distant,
Now it's weighing
On my conscience.

Although I agree,
I call you less often,
Yet sometimes privacy
Is not an option.

I know I made you wait
For our bus ride,
I left my college late,
Just the one time.

Are you now averse
To even holding my hand?
Sometimes it hurts,
And I don't understand.

The other day when
You held me in your arms,

The feeling was alien,
Not sweet or calm.

I felt like I was
Losing myself to you,
So I grasp at straws
To protect my 'selfitude'

But that isn't to say,
That I don't cherish you.
Why would you pull away,
Leaving me confused?

15. Our Tiff

(He)

Yesterday, you and I
Had our first fight.
Life, I can't deny,
Is never cut and dried.

I can't seem to find
The optimum level,
Between a 'never-mind'
And a truly special.

It's hard to fathom
Why you're annoyed,
When I'm the one
Who's been denied,

Affection of any sort.
I take it in my stride,
And try to go along,
Because I have my pride.

But my pride does me
A fat lot of good,

I wallow in my misery,
With a bleak outlook,

I am as lonely as
A fish in a bowl,
Time really drags
For a tormented soul.

16. If Only

(She)

It's now an open secret
That I'm seeing someone,
What this means is that
Speculations have begun.

We ought to be wary,
And measured in everything.
Rumors that carry,
Get under my skin.

I've always been upfront,
And open in my life.
It's all very well when
There's nothing to hide,

But now that I've been
Sneaking around with you,
I can't handle things
With much fortitude.

You keep seeing a
Perfect version of me,

When I'm a normal girl,
With a stubborn streak.

I wish that I could
Keep you to myself,
For, you are my world
And to hell with them!

Just a while longer,
If things stayed as they are,
I'd love you a bit better,
And not ever spar.

17. Come to Me

(He)

My life before you
Was dull and drab,
I was oblivious to
What I didn't have.

To have known you
Is a wonderful thing,
I warily walk through
Where I've never been.

It's a different world
When there's you in it,
This newfound love
Is a novelty to me.

Simple things fascinate you
Like a wide-eyed a child,
How could I refuse
Your enticing, sweet smile?

And so I fell hard,
For your unspoiled ways,

Your innocent charm
Has me rattled and swayed.

I'm glad that you're stuck
With me in a storm,
I haven't seen you enough,
I've waited far too long.

As I hold you tonight,
Close in my arms.
I want you to be mine,
I have you where I want.

18. No Holding Back

(She)

We've stopped meeting
At our usual spots,
Discerning eyes really
Have me overwrought.

Seems there's no place
Left under the sun,
But I need to save face
In front of everyone.

People keep judging us
Wherever we go,
Faces unfamiliar,
And faces I know.

The other day you kissed
Me under a tree.
Can I really blame them
For their audacity?

Where else do we meet,
But at your place?

I'm getting cold feet,
From having fallen from grace.

The storm outside causes
A turbulence within,
As luck would have it,
We are snowed in.

I wrap a scarf I wove,
Around your neck,
We hold each other close,
And it's just perfect!

It's then that I realize,
How much you mean to me,
Without you, my life
Would be pure agony.

It doesn't seem to matter
Now, what anyone thinks,
Even if I get hurt,
I'm going all in.

19. Reality Bites

(He)

The other day I met
Your family over lunch,
I wasn't ready just yet,
But I still took the plunge.

Your presence did offset
My losing side by one,
My chances of success
Though, were zero to none.

Despite my good intentions,
I still lost the game,
I'd hoped for acceptance,
But it was all in vain.

Your father pointed out
The yawning gap between
Our cultures, and disallowed
Any further meetings.

My family also thinks
That you're no match for me,

And that casual flings
Shouldn't be taken seriously.

But I was never with you,
For a bit of good time,
Hurtful meddling tends to
Cause damage and malign.

Meeting you was never
A part of any plan,
It was a sort of fever,
When you and I began.

It wasn't really something
I could stay away from,
I guess that we're destined,
When all is said and done.

It's good that things are
Finally out and in the open,
For a dialogue is, by far,
Better than thoughts unspoken.

Why should we be judged
Through a lens of social norms?
What others think of us?
Why this pressure to conform?

20. The Dilemma

(She)

The real world has
Quite a few norms,
Many can do's and cant's
And rights and wrongs.

Turns out, you and I
Do not make a right,
Various rules apply
In a society civilized.

How could I even
Choose between loves?
One I wasn't seeking,
The other's never enough

My kind, sweet parents
Who gave me life,
And love and care and
Then everything twice!

My moments with you
Shine equally in my mind,

I don't want to lose
Them, or leave your side.

What am I to do,
When nothing seems right?
I don't have a clue,
How to escape my plight.

Can I really leave
One for the other?
Either way I lean,
I'm the one who suffers.

21. Let's Call It Love

(He)

What does it mean
To love someone?
When can you leave?
When are you done?

Is it the shiny new thing,
That makes one's heart race,
When winter feels like spring,
There's a thrill in the chase.

Or is it the enduring kind,
That waits and stays,
That comes with time,
And never goes away.

Is time the test of love,
That makes it profound?
The closeness one dreams of,
And can't do without

Does my love not count
As though it wasn't?

Because it's newfound
Should it be forgotten?

(She)

Your first amorous glance,
Let's call it love.
Then when we met by chance,
Let's call it love.

You sat down beside me,
I joined our names in writing,

When you first held my hand,
Waiting at the bus stand,

Your first peck on my cheek,
When I get weak in the knees,

The desperately long wait,
The one-second hate,

Our first magical kiss,
Our first little tiff,

When I easily forgive,
When we shared everything...

It was all love.

Let's leave it undefined,
And just call it love.
This thing that's yours and mine,
Let's call it love.